SAL'S EATS

SAL'S EATS

SAL'S EATS

Sal's Eats is a full service kitchen where we create American Cuisine. Sal's Eats is a mobile restaurant. We offer menu items such as the Hot Brown Sandwich from Kentucky to Charcuterie boards loaded with fine meats and cheeses. Come experience everything we have to offer at an event or festival near you! Sal's Eats uses locally sourced meats and produce to deliver the highest quality foods from farm to fork. We specialize in menus for wineries and breweries with menus for the whole family.

Event Catering Company

Mobile Kitchen

Event Catering Company Lodi

Lodi Catering Company

#Event Catering Company #Mobile Kitchen #Event Catering Company Lodi #Lodi Catering Company

1341, Lodi, CA 95242

209-609-3291

Contents

CHAPTER ONE

Sal's Eats

Sal's Eats is a full service kitchen where we create American Cuisine. Sal's Eats is a mobile restaurant. We offer menu items such as the Hot Brown Sandwich from Kentucky to Charcuterie boards loaded with fine meats and cheeses. Come experience everything we have to offer at an event or festival near you! Sal's Eats uses locally sourced meats and produce to deliver the highest quality foods from farm to fork. We specialize in menus for wineries and breweries with menus for the whole family.

Event Catering Company

Mobile Kitchen

Event Catering Company Lodi

Lodi Catering Company

#Event Catering Company #Mobile Kitchen #Event Catering Company Lodi #Lodi Catering Company

1341, Lodi, CA 95242

209-609-3291

Sal's Eats is a full service kitchen where we create American Cuisine. Sal's Eats is a mobile restaurant. We offer menu items such as the Hot Brown Sandwich from Kentucky to Charcuterie boards loaded with fine meats and cheeses. Come experience everything we have to offer at an event or festival near you! Sal's Eats uses locally sourced meats and produce to deliver the highest quality foods from farm to fork. We specialize in menus for wineries and breweries with menus for the whole family.

Event Catering Company

Mobile Kitchen

Event Catering Company Lodi

Lodi Catering Company

#Event Catering Company #Mobile Kitchen #Event Catering Company Lodi #Lodi Catering Company

1341, Lodi, CA 95242

209-609-3291

Sal's Eats is a full service kitchen where we create American Cuisine. Sal's Eats is a mobile restaurant. We offer menu items such as the Hot Brown Sandwich from Kentucky to Charcuterie boards loaded with fine meats and cheeses. Come experience everything we have to offer at an event or festival near you! Sal's Eats uses locally sourced meats and produce to deliver the highest quality foods from farm to fork. We specialize in menus for wineries and breweries with menus for the whole family.

Event Catering Company

Mobile Kitchen

Event Catering Company Lodi

Lodi Catering Company

#Event Catering Company #Mobile Kitchen #Event Catering Company Lodi #Lodi Catering Company

1341, Lodi, CA 95242

209-609-3291

Sal's Eats is a full service kitchen where we create American Cuisine. Sal's Eats is a mobile restaurant. We offer menu items such as the Hot Brown Sandwich from Kentucky to Charcuterie boards loaded with fine meats and cheeses. Come experience everything we have to offer at an event or festival near you! Sal's Eats uses locally sourced meats and produce to deliver the highest quality foods from farm to fork. We specialize in menus for wineries and breweries with menus for the whole family.

Event Catering Company

Mobile Kitchen

Event Catering Company Lodi

Lodi Catering Company

#Event Catering Company #Mobile Kitchen #Event Catering Company Lodi #Lodi Catering Company

1341, Lodi, CA 95242

209-609-3291

Sal's Eats is a full service kitchen where we create American Cuisine. Sal's Eats is a mobile restaurant. We offer menu items such as the Hot Brown Sandwich from Kentucky to Charcuterie boards loaded with fine meats and cheeses. Come experience everything we have to offer at an event or festival near you! Sal's Eats uses locally sourced meats and produce to deliver the highest quality foods from farm to fork. We specialize in menus for wineries and breweries with menus for the whole family.

Event Catering Company

Mobile Kitchen

Event Catering Company Lodi

Lodi Catering Company

#Event Catering Company #Mobile Kitchen #Event Catering Company Lodi #Lodi Catering Company

1341, Lodi, CA 95242

209-609-3291

Sal's Eats is a full service kitchen where we create American Cuisine. Sal's Eats is a mobile restaurant. We offer menu items such as the Hot Brown Sandwich from Kentucky to Charcuterie boards loaded with fine meats and cheeses. Come experience everything we have to offer at an event or festival near you! Sal's Eats uses locally sourced meats and produce to deliver the highest quality foods from farm to fork. We specialize in menus for wineries and breweries with menus for the whole family.

Event Catering Company

Mobile Kitchen

Event Catering Company Lodi

Lodi Catering Company

#Event Catering Company #Mobile Kitchen #Event Catering Company Lodi #Lodi Catering Company

1341, Lodi, CA 95242

209-609-3291

Sal's Eats is a full service kitchen where we create American Cuisine. Sal's Eats is a mobile restaurant. We offer menu items such as the Hot Brown Sandwich from Kentucky to Charcuterie boards loaded with fine meats and cheeses. Come experience everything we have to offer at an event or festival near you! Sal's Eats uses locally sourced meats and produce to deliver the highest quality foods from farm to fork. We specialize in menus for wineries and breweries with menus for the whole family.

Event Catering Company

Mobile Kitchen

Event Catering Company Lodi

Lodi Catering Company

#Event Catering Company #Mobile Kitchen #Event Catering Company Lodi #Lodi Catering Company

1341, Lodi, CA 95242

209-609-3291

Sal's Eats is a full service kitchen where we create American Cuisine. Sal's Eats is a mobile restaurant. We offer menu items such as the Hot Brown Sandwich from

Kentucky to Charcuterie boards loaded with fine meats and cheeses. Come experience everything we have to offer at an event or festival near you! Sal's Eats uses locally sourced meats and produce to deliver the highest quality foods from farm to fork. We specialize in menus for wineries and breweries with menus for the whole family.

Event Catering Company

Mobile Kitchen

Event Catering Company Lodi

Lodi Catering Company

#Event Catering Company #Mobile Kitchen #Event Catering Company Lodi #Lodi Catering Company

1341, Lodi, CA 95242

209-609-3291

Sal's Eats is a full service kitchen where we create American Cuisine. Sal's Eats is a mobile restaurant. We offer menu items such as the Hot Brown Sandwich from Kentucky to Charcuterie boards loaded with fine meats and cheeses. Come experience everything we have to offer at an event or festival near you! Sal's Eats uses locally sourced meats and produce to deliver the highest quality foods from farm to fork. We specialize in menus for wineries and breweries with menus for the whole family.

Event Catering Company

Mobile Kitchen

Event Catering Company Lodi

Lodi Catering Company

#Event Catering Company #Mobile Kitchen #Event Catering Company Lodi #Lodi Catering Company

1341, Lodi, CA 95242

209-609-3291

Sal's Eats is a full service kitchen where we create American Cuisine. Sal's Eats is a mobile restaurant. We offer menu items such as the Hot Brown Sandwich from Kentucky to Charcuterie boards loaded with fine meats and cheeses. Come experience everything we have to offer at an event or festival near you! Sal's Eats uses locally sourced meats and produce to deliver the highest quality foods from farm to fork. We specialize in menus for wineries and breweries with menus for the whole family.

Event Catering Company

Mobile Kitchen

Event Catering Company Lodi

Lodi Catering Company

#Event Catering Company #Mobile Kitchen #Event Catering Company Lodi #Lodi Catering Company

1341, Lodi, CA 95242

209-609-3291

Sal's Eats is a full service kitchen where we create American Cuisine. Sal's Eats is a mobile restaurant. We offer menu items such as the Hot Brown Sandwich from Kentucky to Charcuterie boards loaded with fine meats and cheeses. Come experience everything we have to offer at an event or festival near you! Sal's Eats uses locally sourced meats and produce to deliver the highest quality foods from farm to fork. We specialize in menus for wineries and breweries with menus for the whole family.

Event Catering Company

Mobile Kitchen

Event Catering Company Lodi

Lodi Catering Company

#Event Catering Company #Mobile Kitchen #Event Catering Company Lodi #Lodi Catering Company

1341, Lodi, CA 95242

209-609-3291

Sal's Eats is a full service kitchen where we create American Cuisine. Sal's Eats is a mobile restaurant. We offer menu items such as the Hot Brown Sandwich from Kentucky to Charcuterie boards loaded with fine meats and cheeses. Come experience everything we have to offer at an event or festival near you! Sal's Eats uses locally sourced meats and produce to deliver the highest quality foods from farm to fork. We specialize in menus for wineries and breweries with menus for the whole family.

Event Catering Company

Mobile Kitchen

Event Catering Company Lodi

Lodi Catering Company

#Event Catering Company #Mobile Kitchen #Event Catering Company Lodi #Lodi Catering Company

1341, Lodi, CA 95242

209-609-3291

Sal's Eats is a full service kitchen where we create American Cuisine. Sal's Eats is a mobile restaurant. We offer menu items such as the Hot Brown Sandwich from Kentucky to Charcuterie boards loaded with fine meats and cheeses. Come experience everything we have to offer at an event or festival near you! Sal's Eats uses locally sourced meats and produce to deliver the highest quality foods from farm to fork. We specialize in menus for wineries and breweries with menus for the whole family.

Event Catering Company

Mobile Kitchen

Event Catering Company Lodi

Lodi Catering Company

#Event Catering Company #Mobile Kitchen #Event Catering Company Lodi #Lodi Catering Company

1341, Lodi, CA 95242

209-609-3291

Sal's Eats is a full service kitchen where we create American Cuisine. Sal's Eats is a mobile restaurant. We offer menu items such as the Hot Brown Sandwich from Kentucky to Charcuterie boards loaded with fine meats and cheeses. Come experience everything we have to offer at an event or festival near you! Sal's Eats uses locally sourced meats and produce to deliver the highest quality foods from farm to fork. We specialize in menus for wineries and breweries with menus for the whole family.

Event Catering Company

Mobile Kitchen

Event Catering Company Lodi

Lodi Catering Company

#Event Catering Company #Mobile Kitchen #Event Catering Company Lodi #Lodi Catering Company

1341, Lodi, CA 95242

209-609-3291

Sal's Eats is a full service kitchen where we create American Cuisine. Sal's Eats is a mobile restaurant. We offer menu items such as the Hot Brown Sandwich from Kentucky to Charcuterie boards loaded with fine meats and cheeses. Come experience everything we have to offer at an event or festival near you! Sal's Eats uses locally sourced meats and produce to deliver the highest quality foods from farm to fork. We specialize in menus for wineries and breweries with menus for the whole family.

Event Catering Company

Mobile Kitchen

Event Catering Company Lodi

Lodi Catering Company

#Event Catering Company #Mobile Kitchen #Event Catering Company Lodi #Lodi Catering Company

1341, Lodi, CA 95242

209-609-3291

Sal's Eats is a full service kitchen where we create American Cuisine. Sal's Eats is a mobile restaurant. We offer menu items such as the Hot Brown Sandwich from Kentucky to Charcuterie boards loaded with fine meats and cheeses. Come experience everything we have to offer at an event or festival near you! Sal's Eats uses locally sourced meats and produce to deliver the highest quality foods from farm to fork. We specialize in menus for wineries and breweries with menus for the whole family.

Event Catering Company

Mobile Kitchen

Event Catering Company Lodi

Lodi Catering Company

#Event Catering Company #Mobile Kitchen #Event Catering Company Lodi #Lodi Catering Company

1341, Lodi, CA 95242

209-609-3291

Sal's Eats is a full service kitchen where we create American Cuisine. Sal's Eats is a mobile restaurant. We offer menu items such as the Hot Brown Sandwich from Kentucky to Charcuterie boards loaded with fine meats and cheeses. Come experience everything we have to offer at an event or festival near you! Sal's Eats uses locally sourced meats and produce to deliver the highest quality foods from farm to fork. We specialize in menus for wineries and breweries with menus for the whole family.

Event Catering Company

Mobile Kitchen

Event Catering Company Lodi

Lodi Catering Company

#Event Catering Company #Mobile Kitchen #Event Catering Company Lodi #Lodi Catering Company

1341, Lodi, CA 95242

209-609-3291

www.ingramcontent.com/pod-product-compliance
Ingram Content Group UK Ltd.
Pitfield, Milton Keynes, MK11 3LW, UK
UKHW040014200726
13854UKWH00001B/200

9 798888 495568